Retold By: Heather Hamtil
Illustrated By: Patricia F. Braga

ISBN 979-8-9891965-3-1(paperback)

This book is dedicated to the Sacred Heart of Jesus, ever-present in the most Blessed Sacrament, and to all the priests who have generously given their lives to help others know the love of Our Lord, Jesus Christ.

In particular, I dedicate this book to the priests who have personally helped me in this regard — true Spiritual Fathers, patient and kind, ever ready to help any soul entrusted to them.

This is not my own story. Rather, it is based on a true story that was told by a priest on the Feast of Corpus Christi. It is simply retold and illustrated in this book in hopes that children will learn of the example of brave love this child had for Our Lord in the Blessed Sacrament.

Finally, I dedicate this book to my mother who was my first teacher and the most important teacher in my life.
She is also my very best friend. I love her so much.

**arly Days**: This is a true story that took place in a small village in China. A young girl named Li lived in that city, and loved all the things that girls her age would love.

She also had a deep love for learning about Our Lord, ever present in the Most Blessed Sacrament.

**U**nderstanding: It was a Catholic Sister, Sister Euphrasia, who taught the children about Jesus, and prepared them for their First Holy Communion. She taught them that Jesus is present in the consecrated host, the Holy Eucharist.

She explained that this special Bread, the Eucharist, was food for the soul. Li understood how precious this gift was, and she was determined to receive Holy Communion as often as she could.

**risis**: Just like today, there were people who did not love Our Lord. They persecuted those who practiced their Catholic Faith and accused them of superstitious practices.

Li prayed that she would never meet these people, but her prayers were answered differently. One day, angry soldiers stormed the school, yelled at children and took their holy things.

orror: The soldiers forced the people of the village into the tiny church. The soliders shot their guns at the tabernacle..They grabbed the ciborium, containing consecrated Hosts,and and threw them on the floor.

Li watched with horror and wanted to protect Our Lord in the Holy Eucharist.

**ction**: Li's heart broke for Jesus. She wondered why no one was helping Jesus, but they were afraid.

As everyone left the church, Li stayed behind, praying quietly.
She prayed before the Blessed Sacrament.

**isk**: Each day, Li returned to this church and prayed before the Blessed Sacrament. Despite the danger, Li prayed, and at the end of her visit, she would

receive one of the Hosts with her tongue. She did this daily, as the parish priest, Father Luke, watched her from where he was hidden. Amazed at her bravery, he prayed for her safety.

 **ncident:** Finally, there was one consecrated Host left. On that last day, as Li was about to consume the final Host, a soldier saw her, aimed his gun and fired.

Li had been shot, but with all of her strength, she reached for and received the Sacred Host with her tongue.

 **acrifice**: Li made the ultimate sacrifice for Jesus. She died right there, in the church. She was a martyr for her Catholic Faith. The soldier realized what he had done, and was deeply moved by the little girl's love and devotion.

He knew that this young girl's love for Jesus was deep and real. He released the priest so that Li could be buried properly.

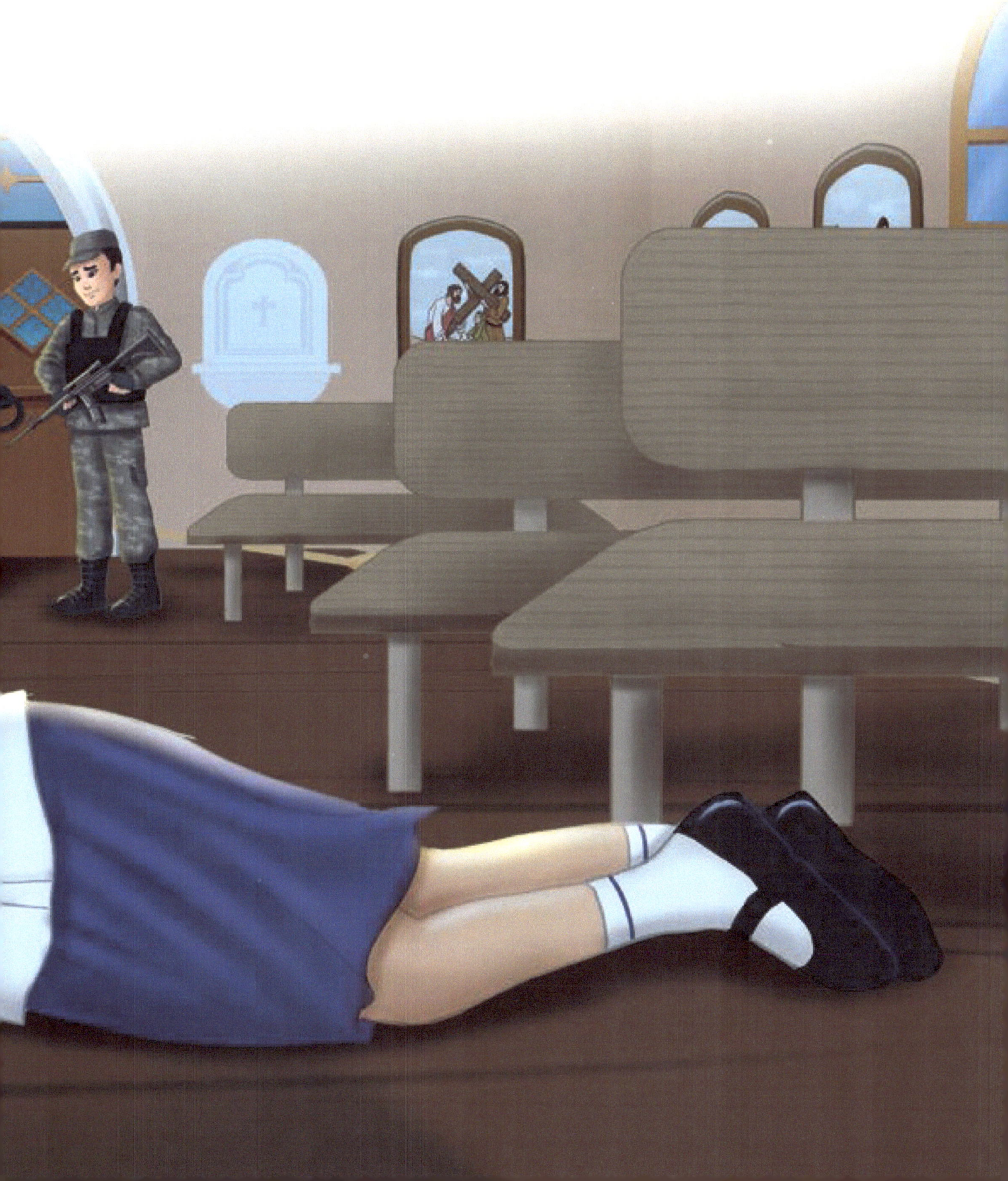

 **imeless**: After Father buried Li, he escaped the village. He shared the story of the young martyr with others. Li's story teaches us all about the importance of the

Most Blessed Sacrament and what a treasure it is to be able to make a Holy Hour with Our Lord.

**nspiration**: Let us pray to have this same love for the Blessed Sacrament, , and let us pray for all of the priests who give their lives so generously.

SANCTUS

They bring Our Lord to us and provide nourishment for our souls.

O Sacrament Most Holy!
O Sacrament Divine!
All praise and all thanksgiving
Be every moment Thine!

**ourage**: As we live our lives and meet with the difficulties of our day, let us pray to have a similar courage as Li did.

Let us live our lives so that others will see Christ in us.

**ove**: Let us love the Most Sacred Heart by remember-ing Him often.

He is our companion and friend, even on our most difficult days.

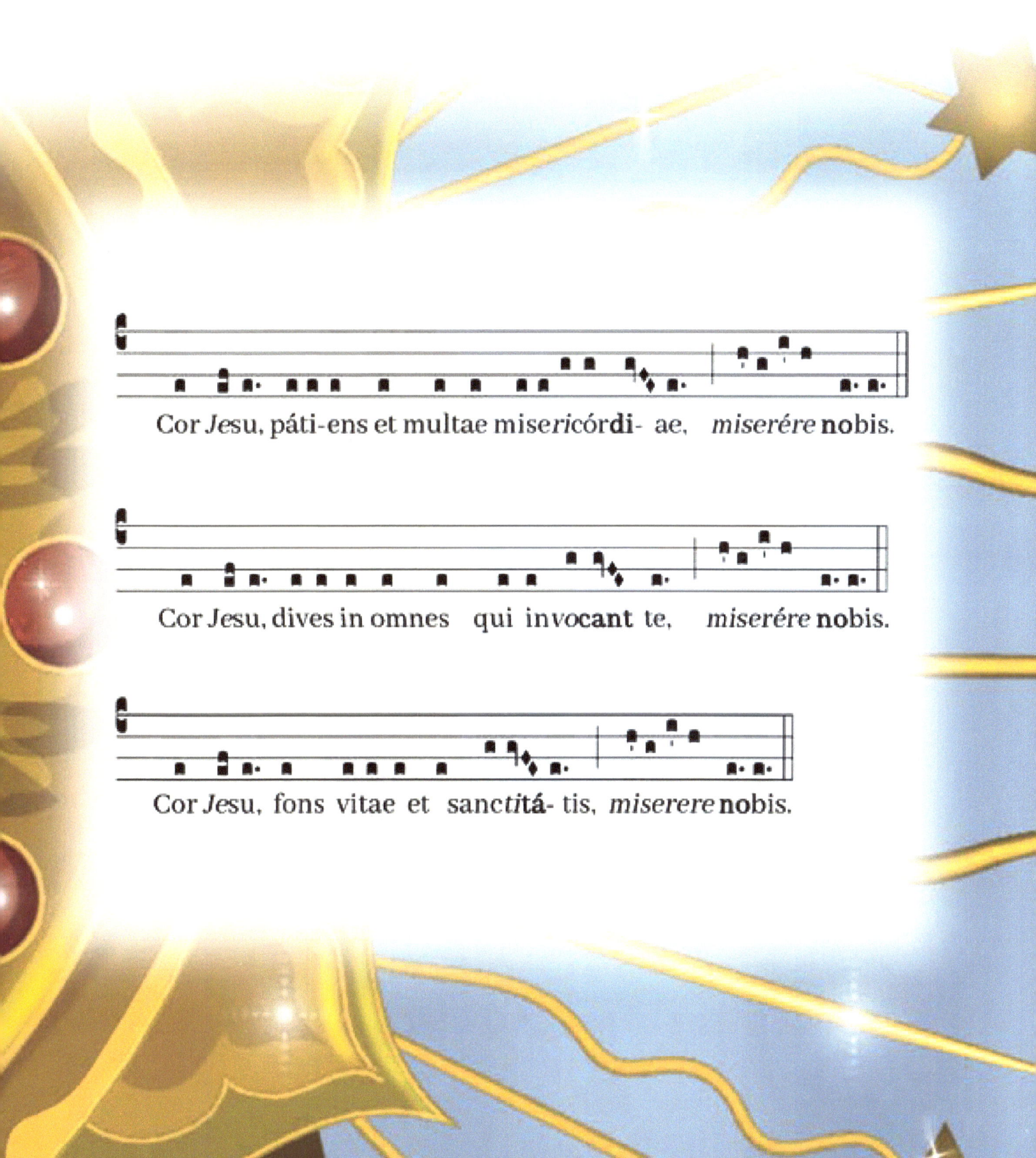

**bedience**: Let us ask God for the courage to obey His Commandments and to live a virtuous life.

Let us be true friends and help others to do the same.

irtue: May this story help you to remember the beautiful gift that God has given to us in the Most Holy Sacrament.

FAITH

HO

Ask God to grant you all the virtues He wishes for you, and may these virtues decorate your life's work.

**ternal:** Although Li did not live a long life, her beautiful story lives on and continues to inspire and teach.

With every Holy Communion that you receive, thank God for His precious gift. It is this gift that will nourish your soul unto life everlasting.

www.ingramcontent.com/pod-product-compliance
Lightning Source LLC
Chambersburg PA
CBHW041605120626
46551CB00002B/317